Can You Hear It?

Can You Hear It?

William Lach

The Metropolitan Museum of Art
Abrams Books for Young Readers • New York

Introduction

Classical music is filled with unforgettable images, from tip-toeing sugarplum fairies to honking Parisian car horns. In this book, we have gathered many great examples of pictorial music and matched them to masterpieces from The Metropolitan Museum of Art, for an introduction to both music and art appreciation for young listeners.

Here, Brueghel's busy winter landscape brings to life Vivaldi's swirling ice skaters, Remington's cowboys depict the gunfire of Copland's *Billy the Kid*, Posada's skeletons rattle their bones to Saint-Saëns's *Fossils*. With this unique book, looking closely at paintings encourages people—especially younger people—to listen closely to music, and vice versa.

The process of choosing appropriate art to illustrate the music varied from piece to piece. With *The Four Seasons*, finding the right art was fairly straightforward, as Vivaldi annotated his score with descriptions of the pictures he had in mind. With *Billy the Kid*, which has no explicit cues, the process was only slightly trickier because the piece was written as a ballet score, and so it has a story outline, scene names, and a performance history. With *The Carnival of the Animals*, which has no cues and was, for the most part, neither published nor publicly performed during the composer's lifetime, the challenge would seem to be greater. However, for this piece—as for all of the others—the score proved an able guide to finding the right picture. We hope you'll agree.

A Note to Parents and Teachers

To play the *Can You Hear It?* game with young listeners, begin by reading the first "Can you hear it?" clue. Then, before you play the CD, ask listeners first to try to find that clue in the picture. (Usually, this first clue will be quite easy to find, but doing so will prepare listeners for hearing it in the music.) Next—with the CD that comes with this book in a nearby player—play the track number listed in one of the upper corners of the image. Then, ask listeners to raise their hands when they hear the right sound effect. (If they have difficulty, you can do it yourself.) Continue on to the follow-up clues, replaying the piece if necessary. (The follow-up clues tend to grow in complexity, and actually "seeing" them in the work of art may require an active imagination!)

After the last clue has been heard, if listeners respond well to a piece, feel free to play it again, and encourage listeners to stand up and act out the pictures the music makes in their heads, as well as those that they see on the page.

To prepare yourself for this book, the front contains a section called "An Introduction to Musical Instruments," which includes beautiful and historically significant examples from The Metropolitan Museum of Art's Department of Musical Instruments. In addition, at the back of the book, a section called "About the Art and Music" contains notes about the artists and composers, as well as interesting facts about the works. A short list of additional educational resources follows that section.

An Introduction to Musical Instruments

This section features many of the musical instruments that can be heard on the CD that comes with this book, as well as some that may be familiar to children. Each instrument is illustrated with an example or picture from the collection of The Metropolitan Museum of Art. While the types of instruments may be well known, the particular examples are quite unusual. Some, like the ivory clarinet, are constructed from rare or precious materials. Others, like the Cristofori piano, are among the oldest of their kind. And some, like the Segovia guitar, were owned and played by famous musicians.

STRINGS

These instruments have strings of different length, thickness, and tightness, made of metal, sheep gut, or nylon, which are stretched over a hollow wooden body. The strings vibrate and sound when they are stroked or tapped with a bow, or plucked and strummed with the fingers or a pick. The hollow body of the instrument amplifies the vibrations, intensifying the sound. String instruments include the violin family, the guitar, the harp, and the zither.

Violin

The versatile violin, pictured at left, is heard in every traditional orchestra, as well as jazz or folk ensembles. A violin player rests the instrument under the chin, supporting the violin's neck with the left hand so that the fingers can "stop" or press the four strings that run the length of the instrument. The violinist holds a bow in the right hand and draws it across the strings, which are held away from the instrument's belly by a piece of carved wood called a bridge. The eighteenth-century Italian craftsman Antonio Stradivari is credited with perfecting the design of the violin, and his instruments are still prized by musicians for their beautiful tone. Stradivari made this violin in 1693, and its fingerboard has been shortened to its original Baroque form.

Violin. Antonio Stradivari, Italian (Cremona), 1644–1737. Wood, L. 23¼ in.

Viola d'amore

The viola d'amore, pictured at left, is similar in shape to the violin. It is also held under the player's chin, but it is larger and has many more strings, which can be adjusted by the additional pegs on the end of the neck. Six or seven strings pass over the bridge and are bowed like those of the violin; the others pass through the bridge and vibrate sympathetically with the bowed strings, giving a shimmery sound to the tone. Composers use the viola d'amore to add a romantic or soulful effect, hence its name "d'amore," meaning "of love."

Viola d'amore. Joseph Gagliano, Italian (Naples), ca. 1780. Wood, L. 14¹¹⁄₁₆ in. (body).

Cello

The cello (short for "violon-cello"), pictured at left, is a member of the violin family. While about twice as large as the violin, it is similar in shape. Both instruments have four strings. The cello's strings are longer and thicker, enabling it to play lower notes. Early cellos were held between the player's legs, but they were later fitted with a metal rod that rests on the floor and supports the instrument. The French maker Vuillaume made this cello in the nineteenth century, as a copy of one made by Antonio Stradivari.

Violoncello. Jean Baptiste Vuillaume, French (Paris), 1798–1875. Wood, L. 29¹¹⁄₁₆ in. (body).

Double Bass

The double bass or bass viol, pictured in the painting above, is the largest and lowest of the bowed strings. It is a member of the viol family; its shoulders are sloped, not rounded like those of the violin and the cello. It may have either four or five strings. The double bass is often heard in symphony orchestras, folk music, and jazz ensembles. Its strings are most often played with a bow, but jazz musicians usually pluck the strings with their fingers.

Dancers in the Rehearsal Room with a Double Bass. Hilaire-Germain-Edgar Degas, French, 1834–1917. Oil on canvas.

Guitar

The guitar, pictured at right, belongs to a family of instruments that includes the lute and the man-dolin. The guitar usually has six strings, a flat back and belly, and a waisted body with one round sound hole. Strips of metal called "frets" are inlaid into the neck to indicate finger placement. The guitar is strummed or plucked. It is a favorite of folk and rock musicians, but it is also used to play classical music. The Spanish guitar master Andrés Segovia launched his career playing this guitar. He recorded with it from 1912 to 1937, and played it at his American debut in 1929.

Classical guitar. Probably Santos Hernández, Spanish (Madrid), 1873–1943, foreman for Manuel Ramirez, Spanish (Madrid), 1864–1916. Wood, L. 18⅝ in. (body).

WOODWINDS

In ancient times, wind instruments were made from bones and reeds, but over time they have been constructed from all sorts of materials—wood, metal, glass, clay, and plastic. Woodwind players direct air into the instrument by blowing over a hole (as for the flute), into a whistle-like mouthpiece (as for the recorder), or through a reed (as for the clarinet, the oboe, the bassoon, and the saxophone). Wind players use their fingers to cover and uncover holes along the instrument's body, or to play keys that cover some holes. They also adjust the pressure of the air that they blow in order to play a range of notes. Wind instruments are often made in sections; on the instruments pictured, the joints indicate how they have been assembled.

Clarinet

The clarinet, pictured at left, has a single reed (a flat, thin section of cane) attached to a mouthpiece with a piece of metal known as a ligature. When the player blows through the mouthpiece, the reed vibrates and the air passing through the instrument also vibrates. The player can produce many different notes by fingering a combination of holes and keys. Modern clarinets are usually made from wood or plastic, but this nineteenth-century example was made from elephant-tusk ivory, once a popular material for wind instruments, but no longer ethically acceptable. Clarinets come in a variety of sizes, from small sopraninos like this one in E-flat to large contrabass clarinets. The size most often seen is the B-flat clarinet, the soprano member of the family, which is a little larger than this one.

Clarinet in E-flat. Theodore Berteling or successor, American (New York), fl. late 19th century. Ivory, nickel-silver, rosewood, L. 18½ in.

Flute

The flute, pictured at left, is essentially a tube open at one end. The musician holds the tube horizontally, blowing air over a single hole on the head joint and fingering the holes and keys on the body of the instrument. Flutes also come in different sizes, with the most commonly seen variation being the piccolo, which plays an octave higher. Claude Laurent, the French clockmaker who designed this flute, obtained a patent for crystal flutes in 1806. Flutes of this period were usually made of wood, but wood can crack, shrink, and warp, so Laurent and others explored materials that were more stable. Today, most modern flutes are made of metal, especially silver and even gold.

Transverse flute in D-flat. Claude Laurent, French (Paris), fl. 1805–1848. Glass and brass, L. 24¾ in.

Oboe

The oboe, pictured at left, developed from the shawm, a Middle Eastern folk instrument that was introduced to Europe in medieval times. Shawms were loud, buzzy instruments used for outdoor music, but the oboe was adapted in the seventeenth century for orchestral and ensemble music. Before being played, this oboe would have received a double reed, made of two thin slices of cane bound tightly together, inserted in the top. Unlike the single reed, which is attached to the mouthpiece, the double reed itself is a mouthpiece, held between the lips while the player blows, to produce a somewhat nasal sound. The oboe has a very consistent pitch, and in the orchestra it usually plays the note to which all the other instruments tune.

Oboe. Jacob Anthony (probably Sr.), American (Philadelphia) (b. Germany), 1736–1804. Boxwood, ivory, and brass, L. 22½ in.

Bassoon

Like the oboe, the bassoon, pictured at left, has a double reed, but its longer size enables it to play lower notes. This example is made of maple and grenadilla, hard and durable woods. The bassoon is actually two tubes joined at the bottom by a U-shape. The player blows air into the instrument through the reed, which is attached to a thin curved metal tube called a bocal. The air passes through one tube to the bottom of the bassoon, then it reverses direction and comes back out through the top, or bell. Frederic Triebert, who made this example, is one of the instrument makers who perfected the modern bassoon.

Bassoon. Frederic Triebert, French (Paris), 1810–ca. 1900. Maple, grenadilla, and brass with gold wash, H. 51½ in.

Saxophone

Like the clarinet, the saxophone, pictured in the collage below, uses a single reed. However, the saxophone's wider reed and cone-shaped bore give it a different sound than the clarinet. Invented by the Belgian Adolphe Sax in about 1840, the saxophone has been played in orchestras and military bands, but has become very popular with jazz musicians. The title of this collage, *The Woodshed*, could refer to the word that musicians use to describe intense practice sessions—*woodshedding*.

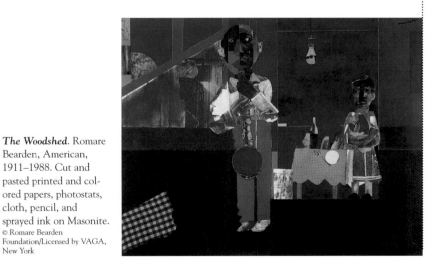

The Woodshed. Romare Bearden, American, 1911–1988. Cut and pasted printed and colored papers, photostats, cloth, pencil, and sprayed ink on Masonite.
© Romare Bearden Foundation/Licensed by VAGA, New York

BRASS

Modern-day brass instruments, most often made of metal, evolved from simple instruments made of animal horns or conch shells that were played as signals and during rituals. Like the woodwinds, brass instruments are somewhat tubular in shape, but their mouthpieces are funnel- or cup-shaped, and they end in a flaring bell for sound amplification. Early orchestral horns were "natural" horns; players had to adjust breath pressure and lip tension to produce different pitches, and they were limited to the notes of the overtone series. With the addition of slides, crooks, and valves to change the length of the tube, brass instruments could play the whole chromatic range of notes. Brass instruments join forces with strings and winds in an orchestra and are also heard in bands and jazz ensembles.

Trumpet

The trumpet, pictured at right, was once commonly made from a long, straight tube of metal, but folding the tube made the instrument more manageable. In the nineteenth century, instrument makers began attaching extra lengths of tubing to the trumpet so it could play a full chromatic range. Three valves pressed by the trumpeter's fingers redirect the air through these tubes. Cornets are similar to trumpets, but they are smaller and have a somewhat different sound.

Valve trumpet in F. Courtois and Mille, French (Paris), ca. 1881. Brass, silver-plated, L. 20½ in.

French Horn

The French horn, pictured at right, is descended from horns used to communicate during hunts. Hunting horns were coiled so that they could be carried over the player's shoulder while he was on horseback. By raising his right arm, he could bring the mouthpiece to his lips while leaving his left arm free to hold the horse's reins. In the nineteenth century, crooks and valves were added to the hunting horn to make it more versatile for orchestral playing. The players hold these horns, not over their shoulders, but on their laps, bell down, and they may insert a hand into the bell as a mute or stop. This instrument was made by the American maker Joseph Lathrop Allen, who is credited with perfecting the rotary type of valve.

Horn. Joseph Lathrop Allen, American (New York), 1815–1897. Brass, L. 16⅚ in.

Euphonium

The euphonium, pictured at left, is a kind of tuba whose name means "sweet voice." This unusual model has two bells—it is actually two instruments in one. The player can alternate between them by pressing on a fifth valve that switches the sound from one instrument to the other. One is louder than the other, and this combination was useful in playing echo effects. An American company that is still manufacturing band instruments made this double-bell euphonium, which is covered with portraits of composers, cartoons, and patriotic symbols. The engraver spent more than two hundred hours engraving and burnishing the instrument, which he gave to his teenage son in 1936.

Double-bell euphonium. C. G. Conn Ltd., American (Elkhart, Indiana), 1936. Metals, H. 31½ in.

Trombone

The trombone, pictured in the detail of the painting at right, uses a moveable slide to lengthen its tube and alter its tone. In Renaissance times, the trombone was known as a sackbut. This painting shows the trombone player as a soloist, standing in front of other musicians who play other wind and brass instruments. Such an ensemble would have been performing a popular tune to attract Parisian visitors to the main event in the tent behind them.

Circus Sideshow (detail). Georges-Pierre Seurat, French, 1859–1891. Oil on canvas.

PERCUSSION

Percussion instruments exist in many forms and sizes, but they all make sounds by being shaken, struck, or scraped. Percussion often provides the rhythm and a constant beat for music and dancing. When added to orchestras, soloists, or small ensembles, they can lend a flavor of the country in which they originated. For example, castanets, pictured in the painting at right, imply a Spanish connection, while the gong evokes Asian music. Percussion instruments include the piano, whose keys set in motion hammers that strike strings; the xylophone, whose tuned bars made of wood, bamboo, or metal are struck or scraped; and the tambourine, which can be struck, scraped, or shaken. Other percussion instruments include the glockenspiel, the kettledrums, and the celeste.

Castanets

Castanets are associated with Spanish music, and they are often played by dancers. Attached to the thumb, the two small, hollowed-out pieces of wood are struck together by the fingers in a rapid staccato beat in time to the music.

Drums

Drums take many sizes and forms throughout the world, but are essentially hollow vessels of metal, wood, clay, or fiberglass, with a membrane of parchment, skin, or plastic stretched over an opening. The membrane is struck with the hands, mallets, or sticks, and the hollow body amplifies the sound. In the orchestra, the bass drum has two drumheads that are struck by soft-headed mallets, one on each side. Tympani, or kettledrums, look like giant metal bowls. They are played in pairs or threes, and they are tuned by foot pedals on each instrument.

Carmencita. William Merritt Chase, American, 1849–1916. Oil on canvas.

Snare Drum

The snare drum, pictured at right, can be played on a stand or worn on the body. It was commonly played in the military to provide a rhythmic pulse for marching soldiers, sometimes accompanied by fifes or bugles. The Union army used this Civil War–era drum, and its wooden frame has been painted with an eagle—a symbol of the United States.

The rope that is wrapped in a zigzag pattern has leather tugs that allow the player to tighten or loosen the drumhead and adjust its pitch. A snare, or string, which runs along the bottom of the drum, rattles as the drum is struck with two sticks.

Side drum. Attributed to Ernest Vogt, American (Philadelphia), ca. 1860. Wood, skin, and rope, H. 15¼ in.

Piano

The piano (short for "pianoforte"), pictured above, was invented by the Italian instrument maker Bartolomeo Cristofori. Unlike its relative the harpsichord, the piano can play both loud and soft notes. (*Piano* means "soft" and *forte* means "loud" in Italian.) When the player depresses keys on the keyboard, hammers strike the strings of steel wire, which in turn vibrate and produce sound. Each key of the piano has its own hammer and course of strings—the short, thin, high strings are on the right and the long, thick, low strings are on the left. The shape of the wooden case reflects the position of the strings that are stretched horizontally inside it. This piano, built by Cristofori in 1720, is considered the oldest piano in the world. Compared with its modern successors, this model is smaller and lighter, and has fewer keys and no pedals.

Pianoforte. Bartolomeo Cristofori, Italian (Florence), 1655–1732. Various materials, L. 90 in.

CAN YOU HEAR
the busy bumblebee flying from flower to flower?

The violins and the flute play the bee at the start of the piece, using many short, quick notes to convey the bee's roundabout flying pattern.

Can you also hear

🎼 the bee hovering above a flower, played by the violins, using lower notes?

🎼 the bee flying again as before, but this time heavy with nectar, played by the clarinets?

ART: **Chrysanthemums**, Utagawa (Andō) Hiroshige, Japanese, 1797–1858. Woodblock print.
MUSIC: **The Flight of the Bumblebee**, Nikolay Rimsky-Korsakov, Russian, 1844–1908.

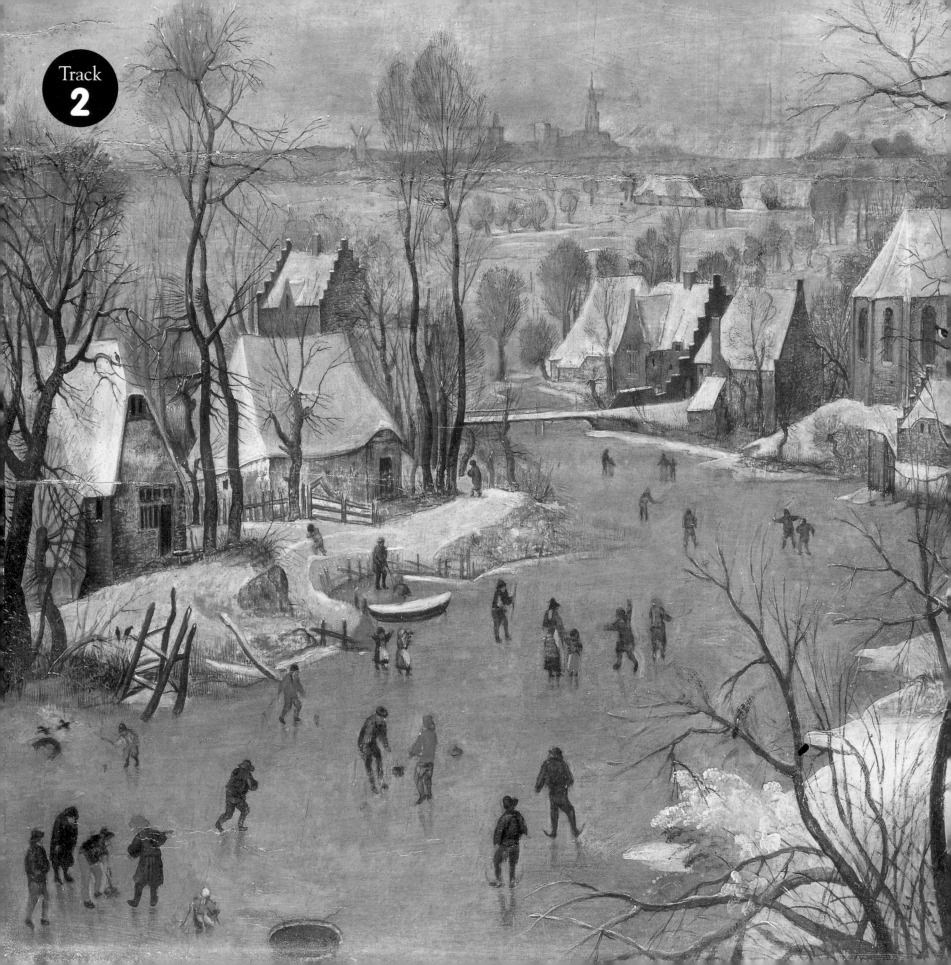

CAN YOU HEAR

the first skater out on the ice, showing off in big loops and figure eights?

The solo violin plays the skater, using quick notes to show the gliding motion.

Can you also hear

♪ a clumsy skater, turning, crashing, and falling, played by the strings— violins, violas, and cellos— quickly moving all the way down the scale?

♪ the North wind blowing hard, played by the solo violin going quickly up and down the scale?

ART: *A Winter Landscape with Skaters and a Bird Trap*, the workshop of Pieter Brueghel the Younger, Flemish, 1564/65–1637/38. Oil on wood.
MUSIC: *The Four Seasons: Winter (Allegro)*, Antonio Vivaldi, Italian, 1678–1741.

CAN YOU HEAR

the passing cars, honking as they rush through crowded city streets?

French horns and actual car horns make these noises.

Can you also hear

𝄞 horses, clomping in and around the traffic, played by the woodblock?

𝄞 people, rushing by on the side-walk, played by the xylophone?

ART: ***Avenue du Bois***, Kees van Dongen, Dutch, 1877–1968. Oil on canvas.
MUSIC: ***An American in Paris*** (excerpt), George Gershwin, American, 1898–1937.

CAN YOU HEAR

the beautiful fish as they swim through the water?

The flute and the violins play the fish, using soft clusters of notes, to show the fishes' graceful movements underwater.

Can you also hear

𝄞 the bubbles, rising to the surface in a zigzag motion, played by the pianos?

𝄞 the sunlight, shining down from above, played by the gentle ringing of the glockenspiel shortly before the end of the piece?

ART: *Ocean Life*, Christian Schussele, American, 1824–1879, and James McAlpin Sommerville, MD, American, 1825–1899. Watercolor, gouache, graphite, and gum arabic on off-white wove paper.
MUSIC: *The Carnival of the Animals: The Aquarium*, Camille Saint-Saëns, French, 1835–1921.

19

CAN YOU HEAR

the marching knights, going off to a tournament?

The violins play the procession of knights moving slowly and steadily.

Can you also hear

♪ the knights' battle call, played by the snare drums?

♪ the armies roaring, played by the trumpets, the trombones, the tubas, and the bass drums?

ART: ***Tournament Book***, unknown artist, German (Nuremberg), late 16th century. Pen and colored wash on paper.
MUSIC: ***Romeo and Juliet: Dance of the Knights*** (excerpt), Sergey Prokofiev, Russian, 1891–1953.

Aº. 1546.   Wolff Andres Linck.

Track
5

4 Varin del et sc.

G. de Gonet édit.

CAN YOU HEAR
the Christmas fairies, tiptoeing out of their hiding places while everyone is asleep?

The violins play the fairies' first steps, with a gentle plucking of the strings.

Can you also hear

♪ the youngest fairies starting to dance, played by the celeste?

♪ the grown-up fairies joining the dance, played by the bass clarinet?

♪ the wands casting magic spells, played by sudden notes from the entire orchestra?

ART: **The Christmas Tree**, Amédée Varin, French, 1818–1883. Hand-colored steel or wood engraving.
MUSIC: **The Nutcracker: Dance of the Sugar Plum Fairy**, Pyotr Illich Tchaikovsky, Russian, 1840–1893.

CAN YOU HEAR
the song of the birds in springtime?

A solo violin, trilling the same high note over and over, plays the birds' song.

Can you also hear

 the mountain stream, played by the entire violin section, softly repeating many short, connected notes?

the thunder, played by the strings—violins, violas, and cellos—quickly repeating the same low note?

ART: **Mountain Torrent**, Jacob van Ruisdael, Dutch, 1628/29–1682. Oil on canvas.
MUSIC: **The Four Seasons: Spring (Allegro)**, Antonio Vivaldi, Italian, 1678–1741.

CAN YOU HEAR
the rattling skeletons, dancing to the music of the orchestra?

The xylophone—looking something like a bunch of bones itself—plays the skeletons.

Can you also hear

🎼 the skeletons, played again by the xylophone, striking their own bones as an accompaniment, while the pianos and strings take the lead?

🎼 a bit of the song "Twinkle, Twinkle, Little Star," played by the piano? (This is one of the composer's jokes—"Twinkle, Twinkle" is an old tune that will never die, and so it, too, is something of a skeleton!)

ART: **The Calavera of Cupid** (details), José Guadalupe Posada, Mexican, 1852–1913. Zinc etching, type-metal, and letterpress on paper.
MUSIC: **The Carnival of the Animals: Fossils**, Camille Saint-Saëns, French, 1835–1921.

CAN YOU HEAR
one cat meowing when it sees the spilled milk?

A female opera singer known as a mezzo-soprano sings the first cat.

Can you also hear

🎼 a second cat joining in with the first, sung by a soprano opera singer (slightly higher than the first)?

🎼 the cats hissing when they get too close, also sung by the opera singers?

🎼 the cats purring when their bellies are full, again sung by the opera singers?

ART: **My Little White Kitties into Mischief**, published by Currier and Ives, American, active 1852–1907. Hand-colored lithograph.
MUSIC: **Comic Duet for Two Cats**, attributed to Gioachino Rossini, Italian, 1792–1868.

CAN YOU HEAR
the enormous elephant?

The double bass plays the animal.

Can you also hear

♪ the elephant doing the delicate dance known as the waltz, to a beat of ONE two-three, ONE two-three, ONE two-three?

♪ the elephant swaying and gliding, with higher and longer notes than before, in the middle of the piece?

ART: *Prince Riding on an Elephant*, Khem Karan, Indian, Mughal period, 16th–17th century. Ink, opaque watercolor, and gold on paper.
MUSIC: *The Carnival of the Animals: The Elephant*, Camille Saint-Saëns, French, 1835–1921.

CAN YOU HEAR
the gun battle?

The kettledrums play the gunfire.

Can you also hear

♪ the outlaw scrambling for cover, played by the trumpets?

♪ the men marching the outlaw back to town at the end of the piece, played by the bass drum and the piano?

ART: **On the Southern Plains**, Frederic Remington, American, 1861–1909. Oil on canvas.
MUSIC: **Billy the Kid: Gun Battle**, Aaron Copland, American, 1900–1990.

CAN YOU HEAR
the sudden thunder in the summer storm?

The strings—violins, violas, and cellos—play the thunder at the start of the piece, repeating the same low note very quickly.

Can you also hear

♪ the trees being blown by the wind, played by all the violins going quickly down the scale?

♪ a bird trying to find shelter, played by the solo violin playing very high, quick notes?

ART: *View from Mount Holyoke, Northampton, Massachusetts, After a Thunderstorm—The Oxbow*, Thomas Cole, American (b. England), 1801–1848. Oil on canvas.
MUSIC: *The Four Seasons: Summer (Presto)*, by Antonio Vivaldi, Italian, 1678–1741.

All of the works of art reproduced in this book are from the collection of The Metropolitan Museum of Art.

TITLE PAGE: *Circus Sideshow*. Georges-Pierre Seurat, French, 1859–1891. Oil on canvas. Bequest of Stephen C. Clark, 1960 61.101.17

PAGE 4: *The Love Song* (detail). Sir Edward Coley Burne-Jones, English, 1833–1898. Oil on canvas. The Alfred N. Punnett Endowment Fund, 1947 47.26

PAGE 5: *The Violinist* (detail). Hilaire-Germain-Edgar Degas, French, 1834–1917. Pastel and charcoal on green paper, squared for transfer. Rogers Fund, 1918 19.51.1

Published by The Metropolitan Museum of Art, New York, and Harry N. Abrams, Inc., New York

First Edition
Printed in Malaysia
10 09 08   10 9 8 7 6 5

Produced by the Department of Special Publications, The Metropolitan Museum of Art: Robie Rogge, Publishing Manager; William Lach, Senior Editor; Mimi Tribble, Assistant Editor; Anna Raff, Designer; Mahin Kooros, Production Associate.
All photography by The Metropolitan Museum of Art Photograph Studio

"An Introduction to Musical Instruments" was written by Rebecca Arkenberg, in cooperation with the Department of Musical Instruments, The Metropolitan Museum of Art.

Visit the Museum's website: www.metmuseum.org

Library of Congress Cataloging-in-Publication data has been applied for.

ISBN 10 (MMA): 1-58839-182-5
ISBN 13 (MMA): 978-1-58839-182-7
ISBN 10 (Abrams): 0-8109-5721-3
ISBN 13 (Abrams): 978-0-8109-5721-3

HNA ▪▪▪▪▪
harry n. abrams, inc.
a subsidiary of La Martinière Groupe
115 West 18th Street
New York, NY 10011
www.hnabooks.com

About the Art and Music

THE BUSY BUMBLEBEE pages 12–13
ART: *Chrysanthemums*, Utagawa (Andō) Hiroshige
MUSIC: *The Flight of the Bumblebee*, Nikolay Rimsky-Korsakov

Hiroshige is one of the most famous Japanese woodblock printmakers. Each of his prints required carving up to twenty separate blocks of cherry wood, one for each color in the design. Note the curved outline of this image—it was probably designed for use as a fan. **Rimsky-Korsakov** led a dual life as a young man, working as a sailor as well as a composer, buying musical scores at ports from London to Rio de Janeiro. This piece, from his fairy-tale opera *The Tale of Tsar Saltan*, is an orchestral interlude meant to grab the audience's attention.

H. O. Havemeyer Collection, Bequest of Mrs. H. O. Havemeyer, 1929 JP 1899

THE FIRST SKATER pages 14–15
ART: *A Winter Landscape with Skaters and a Bird Trap*, the workshop of Pieter Brueghel the Younger
MUSIC: *The Four Seasons: Winter (Allegro)*, Antonio Vivaldi

Brueghel is called "the Younger" because his father was also a painter named Pieter. In fact, Brueghel the Younger is primarily known for running a workshop that made copies of the pictures of his more well-known father. This painting is one of sixty versions he made, all based on the same work. **Vivaldi** grew up in Venice and learned to play the violin as a boy, probably from his father, who was both a violinist and a barber. He began his career as the music master at an orphanage and school for girls, but soon became known for his compositions, many of which became bestsellers.

Bequest of Grace Wilkes, 1921 22.45.5

THE PASSING CARS pages 16–17
ART: *Avenue du Bois*, Kees van Dongen
MUSIC: *An American in Paris* (excerpt), George Gershwin

Van Dongen moved to Paris in 1897 and was initially very poor, supporting himself for a time as a circus wrestler. By 1910, he was a great success as an artist. Eventually, he became known for his portraits of society figures and celebrities. **Gershwin** was born in Brooklyn and achieved early success, first composing popular sheet music, then Broadway musicals, and finally orchestral works. He wrote *An American in Paris* during a trip to that city. This excerpt depicts Paris by day; later segments depict Paris by night and at dawn.

Robert Lehman Collection, 1975 1975.1.227

THE BEAUTIFUL FISH pages 18–19
ART: *Ocean Life*, Christian Schussele and James McAlpin Sommerville, MD
MUSIC: *The Carnival of the Animals: The Aquarium*, Camille Saint-Saëns

Schussele was the first professor in drawing and painting at the Pennsylvania Academy of the Fine Arts; **Sommerville** was a trustee there and an amateur naturalist. Crammed with more than seventy-five examples of seaweed, urchins, crustaceans, and fish from subtropical waters, this painting conveys a strong sensation of ocean life although not a literal representation of it. **Saint-Saëns** learned to play the piano at age three and began performing his own compositions at age ten. In *The Aquarium*, Saint-Saëns's billowing melody and plinking piano keys prompt an "aha" of recognition—like Schussele and Sommerville's painting—despite the fact that the sea is a largely silent world.

Gift of Mr. and Mrs. Erving Wolf, 1977 1977.181

THE MARCHING KNIGHTS pages 20–21
ART: *Tournament Book*, unknown artist, German (Nuremberg), late 16th century
MUSIC: *Romeo and Juliet: Dance of the Knights* (excerpt), Sergey Prokofiev

An unknown German artist from the late sixteenth century created this illuminated manuscript, which shows knights in tournament armor and fanciful costume. It was created during roughly the same period that Shakespeare wrote his play *Romeo and Juliet*, the source of this early-twentieth-century ballet. **Prokofiev** was born in Ukraine, and his artistic career, though fruitful, occasionally mirrored his homeland's tumultuous history. In the ballet *Romeo and Juliet*, the knights meet at a dance, not a battle, but Prokofiev strongly suggests their tours of duty with the piece's minor tones and the rat-a-tat-tat of that instrumental call to arms, the snare drum.

Rogers Fund, 1922 22.229

THE CHRISTMAS FAIRIES page 22
ART: *The Christmas Tree*, Amédée Varin
MUSIC: *The Nutcracker: Dance of the Sugar Plum Fairy*, Pyotr Illich Tchaikovsky

Varin was born into a family of artists, and in this illustration—as in Tchaikovsky's ballet—the Victorian transformation of Yuletide into a family holiday is evident, with toys and a decorated tree, and with children playing a central role. **Tchaikovsky** was Russia's first professional full-time composer. Today, his popularity ranks among the highest, and no less so than with his ballet *The Nutcracker*, in which a little girl falls asleep under the tree on Christmas Eve and dreams of a land of dancing sweets, guided by the Sugar Plum Fairy.

Gift of Lincoln Kirstein, 1970 1970.565.31

THE SONG OF THE BIRDS page 23

ART: *Mountain Torrent*, Jacob van Ruisdael
MUSIC: *The Four Seasons: Spring (Allegro)*, Antonio Vivaldi

Ruisdael was one of the most important landscape painters in Europe during the seventeenth century and was highly admired in Vivaldi's day. Naturalistic landscape painting flourished in the Netherlands from the 1620s onward, and was encouraged by trade, exploration, and the study of natural sciences. This canvas depicts Scandinavian topography, which enjoyed a vogue in Amsterdam during the second half of the 1600s. **Vivaldi** is best known for *The Four Seasons*, which, like the year, contains four parts, each divided into three smaller parts. This piece is its best-known movement.

Bequest of Collis P. Huntington, 1900 25.110.18

THE RATTLING SKELETONS pages 24–25

ART: *The Calavera of Cupid*, José Guadalupe Posada
MUSIC: *The Carnival of the Animals: Fossils*, Camille Saint-Saëns

Posada is a founding figure in Mexico's popular art tradition, creating prints for inexpensively printed flyers, often political in nature. His audience was the poor and illiterate, and his targets were often the powerful. For this, he was frequently imprisoned. He is best known for his animated skeletons, known as *calaveras*, inspired by figures from the Mexican Day of the Dead celebration. **Saint-Saëns**'s piece shows off the bonelike xylophone. Although his piece celebrates fossils, not skeletons, the composer himself made the xylophone/skeleton comparison in his longer work *Danse Macabre*.

The Elisha Whittelsey Collection, The Elisha Whittelsey Fund, 1946 46.46.308

ONE CAT MEOWING pages 26–27

ART: *My Little White Kitties into Mischief*, Currier and Ives
MUSIC: *Comic Duet for Two Cats*, attributed to Gioachino Rossini

Currier and Ives, a New York lithography firm, produced prints of thousands of subjects and controlled three-quarters of the American market in the latter half of the nineteenth century. Printed in black and white, most of the pictures were filled in with watercolors by women working from home. **Rossini** was born to musicians in a small city on the Adriatic Sea. He began singing professionally by age twelve, and composing at eighteen. Known as the greatest Italian composer of his time, he is beloved for his comic operas. Current scholarship doubts whether he wrote this piece, but not its sense of humor.

Bequest of Adele S. Colgate, 1962 63.550.479

THE ENORMOUS ELEPHANT pages 28–29

ART: *Prince Riding on an Elephant*, Khem Karan
MUSIC: *The Carnival of the Animals: The Elephant*, Camille Saint-Saëns

Karan, an artist at the court of the Mughal emperor Akbar, produced this painting. Akbar, who inherited the throne at age twelve, gathered to his court some thirty artists and seventy assistants, from various cultures. This painting reflects this diversity, with influences such as Persian (in the Prince's face), Mughal (in the elephant's depth), and indigenous Indian (in the coloration). **Saint-Saëns** wrote *Carnival* in a few days, while on vacation in Austria. He allowed only one small part of it to be published and publicly performed in his lifetime, probably because he thought the entire symphony too frivolous. It has become his most beloved work.

Rogers Fund, 1925 25.68.4

THE GUN BATTLE pages 30–31

ART: *On the Southern Plains*, Frederic Remington
MUSIC: *Billy the Kid: Gun Battle*, Aaron Copland

Remington, a painter and sculptor, traveled through the West for artistic inspiration, but spent most of his working life back East, in and outside of New York City. The dynamic brushstrokes and bright colors in this painting show the influence of Impressionism upon his later work. **Copland** was born in Brooklyn to parents who owned a department store. He frequently used American themes in his work and eventually became known as America's greatest living composer. The real Billy the Kid was an infamous outlaw who was also born in New York City.

Gift of Several Gentlemen, 1911 11.192

THE SUDDEN THUNDER pages 32–33

ART: *View from Mount Holyoke, Northampton, Massachusetts, After a Thunderstorm—The Oxbow*, Thomas Cole
MUSIC: *The Four Seasons: Summer (Presto)*, Antonio Vivaldi

Cole moved to America from an industrial city in England when he was eighteen. Inspired by the grandeur and wilderness of the American landscape, he became the most prominent figure in the group of painters now known as the Hudson River School. In the lower-central part of this canvas, Cole depicted himself, at an easel. **Vivaldi** published the score of *The Four Seasons* with sonnets for his audience and cues for his musicians so that they would know precisely what sounds they were hearing or playing.

Gift of Mrs. Russell Sage, 1908 08.228

THE MUSICIANS back cover
ART: *Circus Sideshow*, Georges-Pierre Seurat
MUSIC: *The Carnival of the Animals: Finale*, Camille Saint-Saëns

Seurat developed the technique of painting with many small dots, known as Pointillism. This painting shows the free entertainment offered at the entrance of a traveling theater to lure in customers. It was Seurat's first attempt to use Pointillism to render the effects of artificial light at night. **Saint-Saëns** was the first established classical composer to write for the movies (*L'assassinat du duc de Guise*, 1908), which is fitting, since this piece and other works by him so masterfully create a virtual picture in the listener's mind.

Bequest of Stephen C. Clark, 1960 61.101.17

Educational Resources

The Metropolitan Museum of Art's Department of Musical Instruments contains the largest and most comprehensive collection of its kind outside Europe. The Museum's André Mertens Galleries for Musical Instruments are located on the second floor of the Museum, above the Emma and Georgina Bloomberg Arms and Armor Court. The galleries display instruments from around the world, including those depicted in this book.

The Metropolitan Museum of Art's website, www.metmuseum.org, and many Metropolitan Museum publications provide information about art, artists, and musical instruments. Additional resources follow:

Grove Art Online. Oxford University Press. www.groveart.com.
Grove Music Online, ed. L. Macy. www.grovemusic.com.
The Oxford Companion to Western Art, ed. Hugh Brigstocke, Oxford University Press, 2001.
The Instruments of the Orchestra (compact disc). Written and narrated by Jeremy Siepmann, Naxos 8.558040-46, ℗ and © 2002 HNH International Ltd.

Art Credits

PAGE 6: **Violin**, Gift of George Gould, 1955 55.86a-c
Viola d'amore, Gift of Hans H. Schambach, 1981 1981.480

PAGE 7: **Violoncello**, Gift of Peter Blos, 1984 1984.114.1
Dancers in the Rehearsal Room with a Double Bass, H. O. Havemeyer
Collection, Bequest of Mrs. H. O. Havemeyer, 1929 29.100.127
Classical guitar, Gift of Emilita Segovia, Marquessa of Salobreña, 1986 1986.353.2

PAGE 8: **Clarinet in E-flat**, Rogers Fund, 1982 1982.18
Transverse flute in D-flat, The Crosby Brown Collection of Musical
Instruments, 1889 89.4.924
Oboe, Purchase, Gift of Albany Institute of History and Art, by exchange, and
Rogers Fund, 1997 1997.272
Bassoon, Purchase, Clara Mertens Bequest, in memory of André Mertens,
2003 2003.49a-h

PAGE 9: *The Woodshed*, George A. Hearn Fund, 1970 1970.19
Valve trumpet in F, Purchase, Bequest of Robert Alonzo Lehman, by exchange,
2001 2001.187a-i

PAGE 10: **Horn**, The Crosby Brown Collection of Musical Instruments, 1889
89.4.2198
Double-bell euphonium, Purchase, Werner Kramarsky Gift, 1989 1989.322
Circus Sideshow (detail), Bequest of Stephen C. Clark, 1960 61.101.17

PAGE 11: *Carmencita*, Gift of Sir William Van Horne, 1906 06.969
Side drum, The Crosby Brown Collection of Musical Instruments, 1889 89.4.2162
Pianoforte, The Crosby Brown Collection of Musical Instruments, 1889 89.4.1219

Recording Credits

This enclosed audio recording ℗ and © 2006 Classical Communications Ltd.
Following are credits for the individual tracks on the recording.

1. Rimsky-Korsakov, *The Flight of the Bumblebee*
The Camerata Rhenania, conducted by Hanspeter Gmür

2. Vivaldi, *The Four Seasons: Winter (Allegro)*
Pavel Popov, violin, the St. Petersburg Radio and Television Orchestra, conducted
by Stanislav Gorvenko

3. Gershwin, *An American in Paris* (excerpt)
The Orlando Pops Orchestra, conducted by Andrew Lane

4. Saint-Saëns, *The Carnival of the Animals: The Aquarium*
Marylene Dosse and Anne Petit, piano, the Württemberg Chamber Orchestra,
conducted by Jörg Faerber

5. Prokofiev, *Romeo and Juliet: Dance of the Knights* (excerpt)
The Minnesota Orchestra, conducted by Stanislaw Skrowaczewski

6. Tchaikovsky, *The Nutcracker: Dance of the Sugar Plum Fairy*
The London Symphony Orchestra, conducted by Don Jackson

7. Vivaldi, *The Four Seasons: Spring (Allegro)*
Pavel Popov, violin, the St. Petersburg Radio and Television Orchestra, conducted
by Stanislav Gorvenko

8. Saint-Saëns, *The Carnival of the Animals: Fossils*
Marylene Dosse and Anne Petit, piano, the Württemberg Chamber Orchestra,
conducted by Jörg Faerber

9. Attributed to Rossini, *Comic Duet for Two Cats*
Sara Stowe and Penelope Martin-Smith, accompanied by Matthew Spring

10. Saint-Saëns, *The Carnival of the Animals: The Elephant*
Marylene Dosse and Anne Petit, piano, the Württemberg Chamber Orchestra,
conducted by Jörg Faerber

11. Copland, *Billy the Kid: Gun Battle*
The Dallas Symphony Orchestra, conducted by Donald Johanos

12. Vivaldi, *The Four Seasons: Summer (Presto)*
Pavel Popov, violin, the St. Petersburg Radio and Television Orchestra, conducted
by Stanislav Gorvenko

13. Saint-Saëns, *The Carnival of the Animals: Finale*
Marylene Dosse and Anne Petit, piano, the Württemberg Chamber Orchestra,
conducted by Jörg Faerber

All of the works of art reproduced in this book are from the collection of The Metropolitan Museum of Art.

TITLE PAGE: *Circus Sideshow*. Georges-Pierre Seurat, French, 1859–1891. Oil on canvas. Bequest of Stephen C. Clark, 1960 61.101.17

PAGE 4: *The Love Song* (detail). Sir Edward Coley Burne-Jones, English, 1833–1898. Oil on canvas. The Alfred N. Punnett Endowment Fund, 1947 47.26

PAGE 5: *The Violinist* (detail). Hilaire-Germain-Edgar Degas, French, 1834–1917. Pastel and charcoal on green paper, squared for transfer. Rogers Fund, 1918 19.51.1

Published by The Metropolitan Museum of Art, New York, and Harry N. Abrams, Inc., New York

First Edition
Printed in Malaysia
10 09 08   10 9 8 7 6 5

Produced by the Department of Special Publications, The Metropolitan Museum of Art: Robie Rogge, Publishing Manager; William Lach, Senior Editor; Mimi Tribble, Assistant Editor; Anna Raff, Designer; Mahin Kooros, Production Associate.
All photography by The Metropolitan Museum of Art Photograph Studio

"An Introduction to Musical Instruments" was written by Rebecca Arkenberg, in cooperation with the Department of Musical Instruments, The Metropolitan Museum of Art.

Visit the Museum's website: www.metmuseum.org

Library of Congress Cataloging-in-Publication data has been applied for.

ISBN 10 (MMA): 1-58839-182-5
ISBN 13 (MMA): 978-1-58839-182-7
ISBN 10 (Abrams): 0-8109-5721-3
ISBN 13 (Abrams): 978-0-8109-5721-3

HNA
harry n. abrams, inc.
a subsidiary of La Martinière Groupe
115 West 18th Street
New York, NY 10011
www.hnabooks.com